I0475210

www.facebook.com/littleflatbear

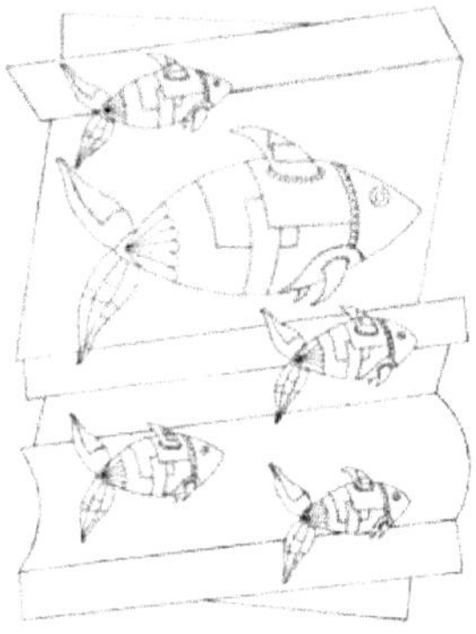
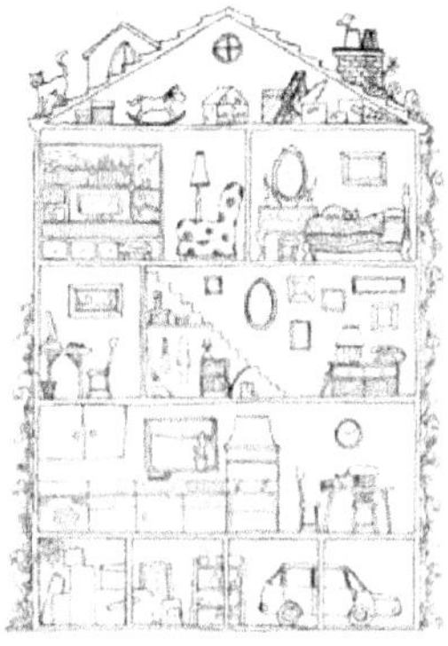
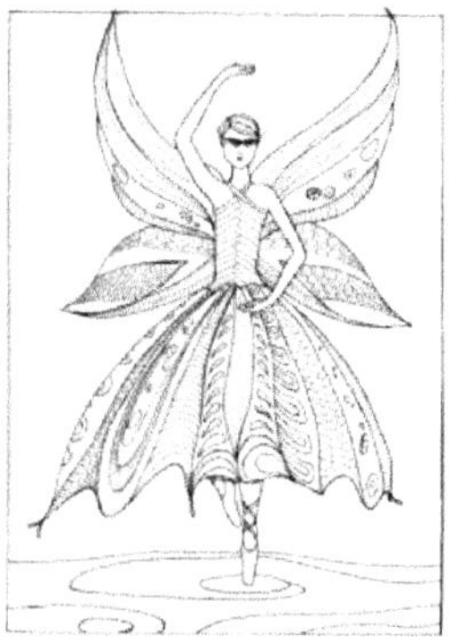
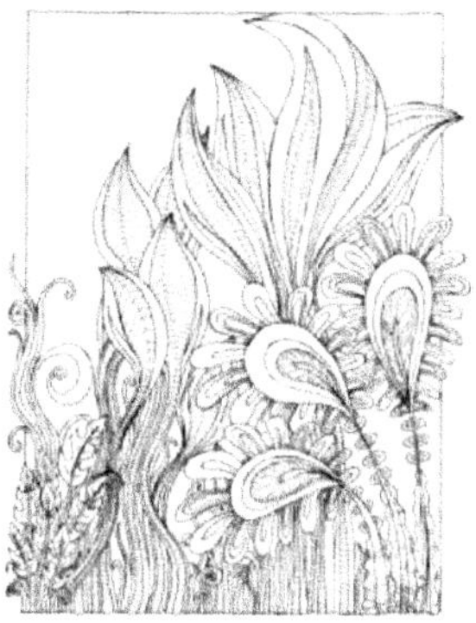
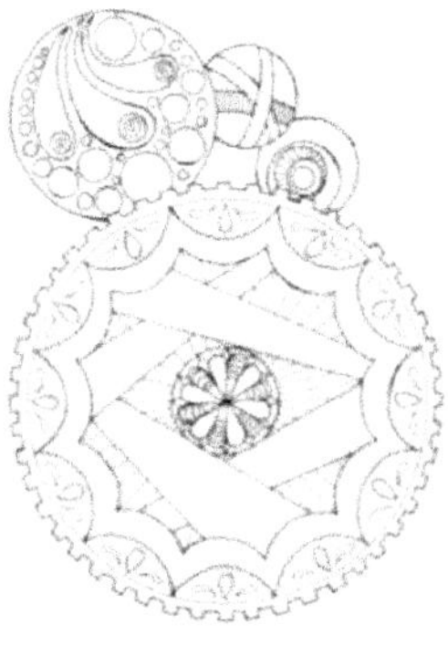
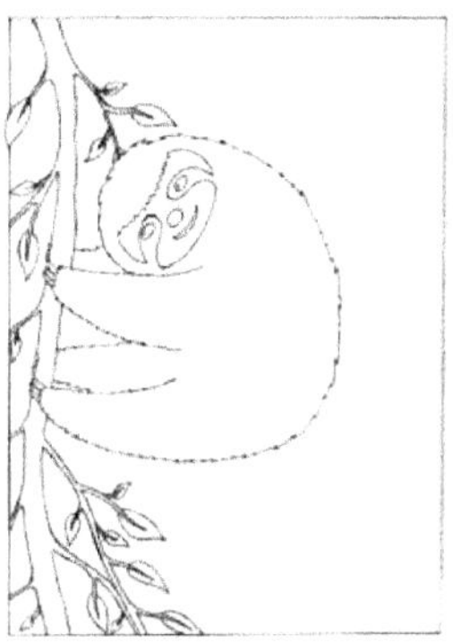
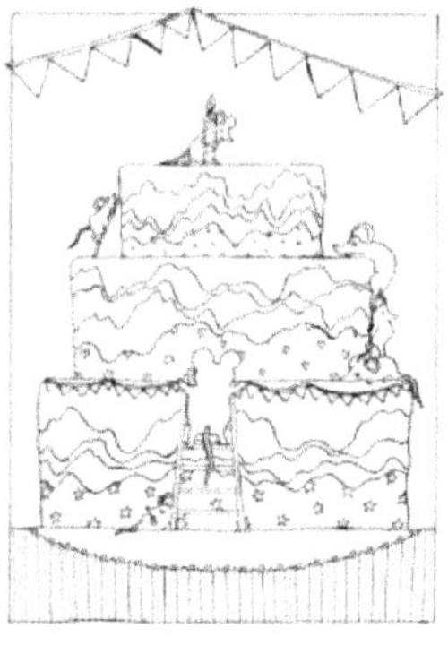
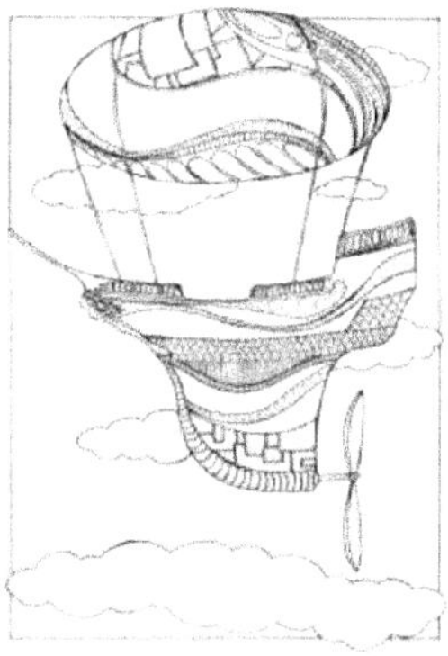
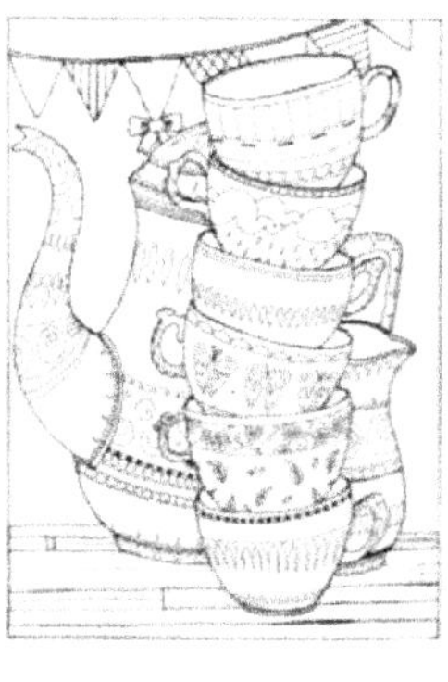
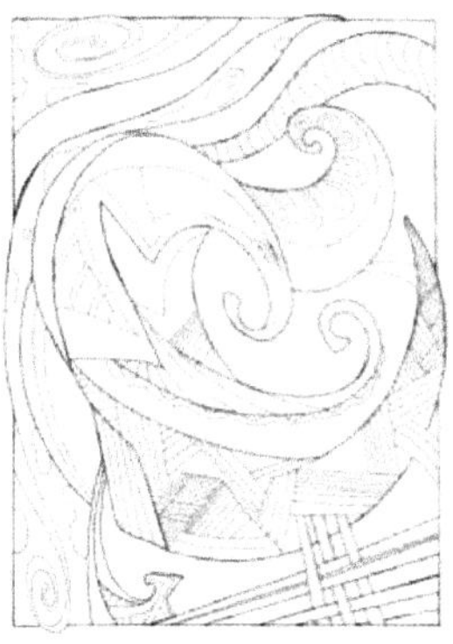
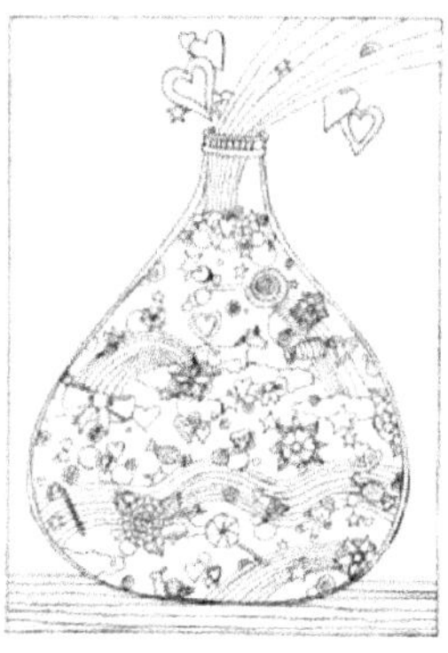
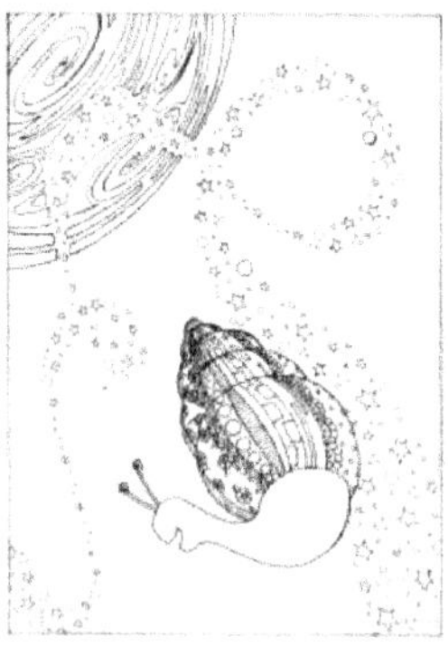

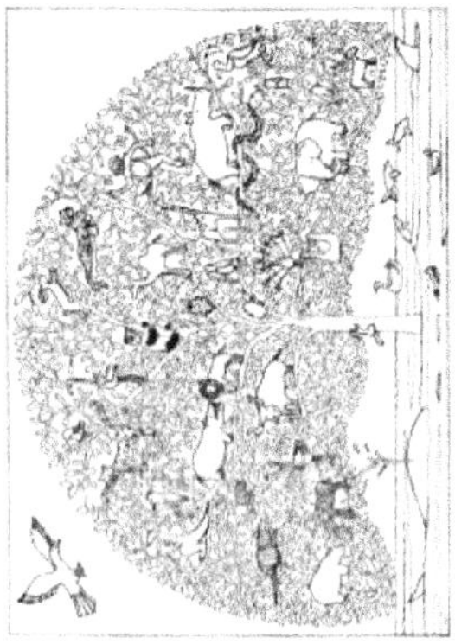
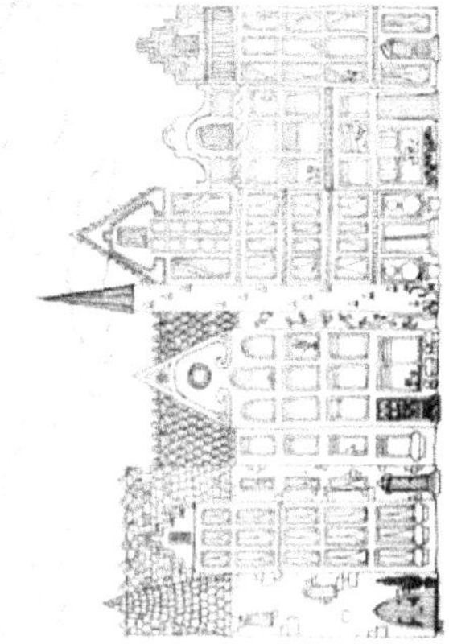
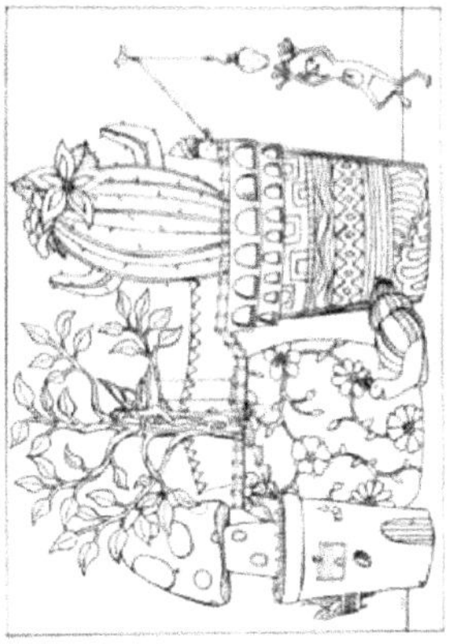
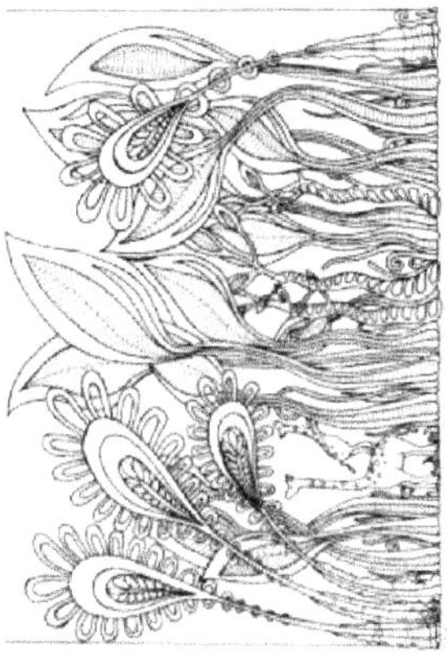
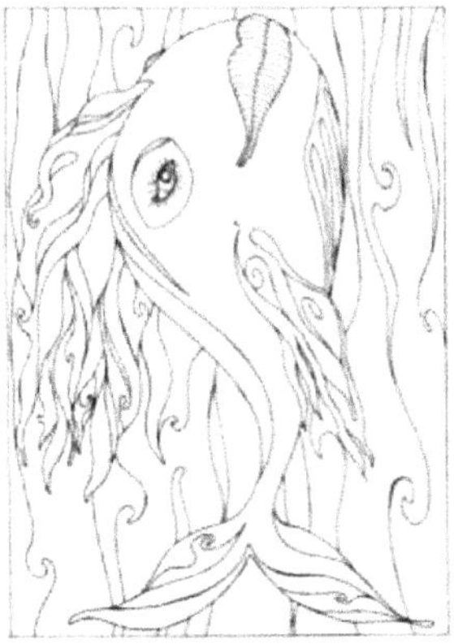
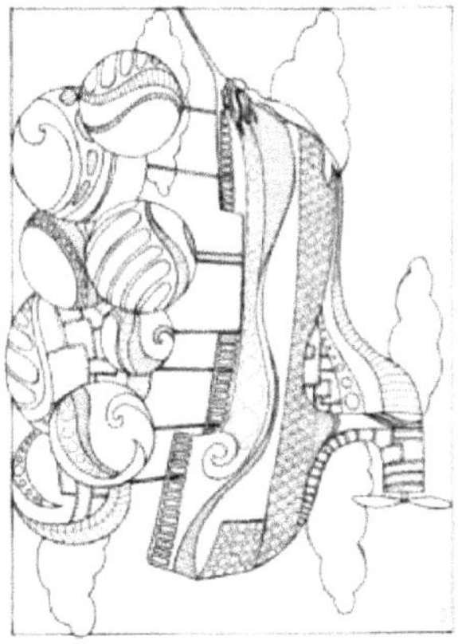
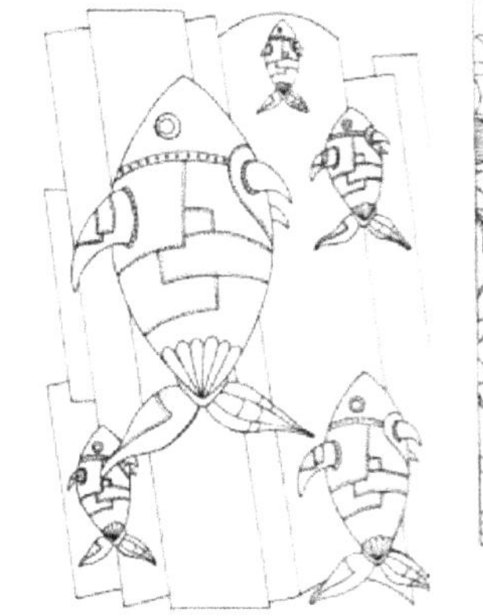
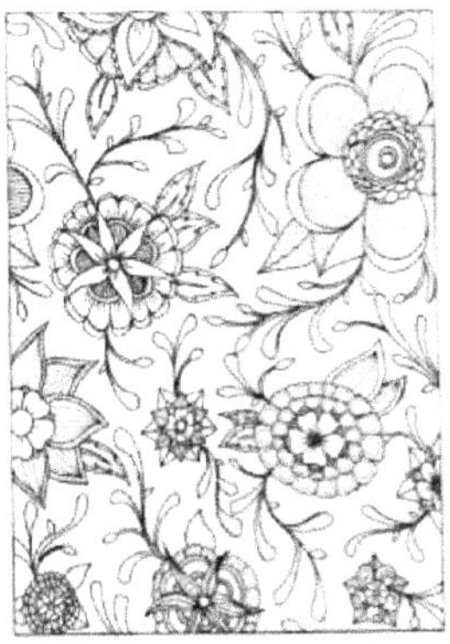
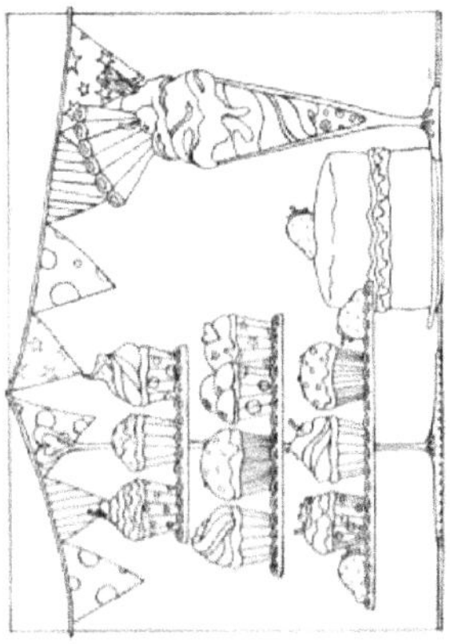
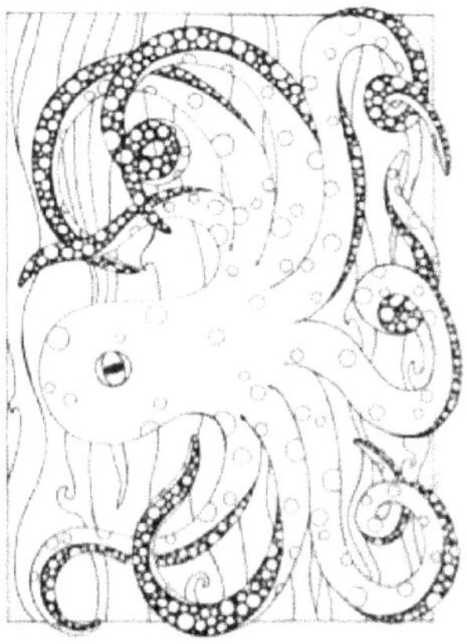
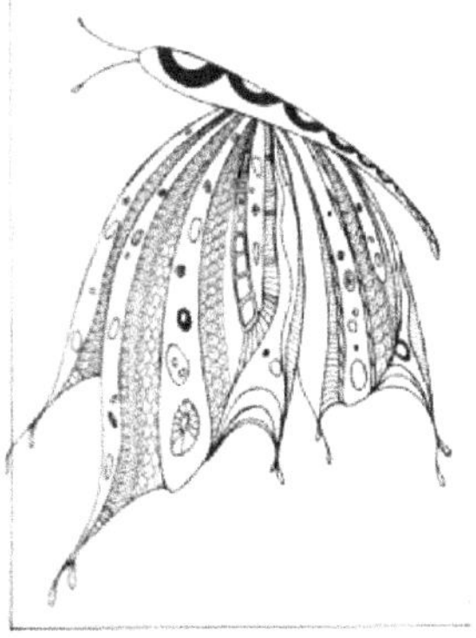
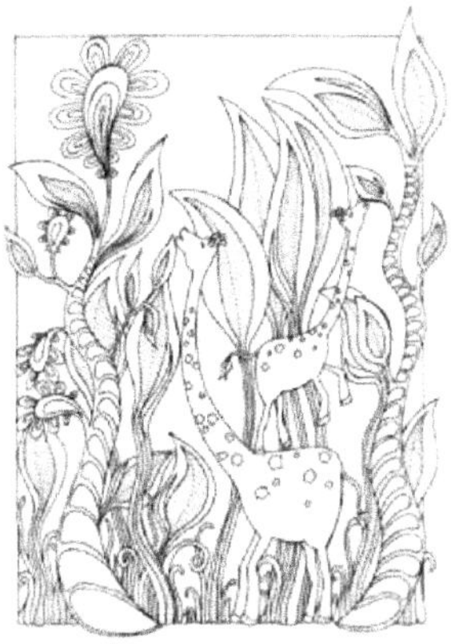

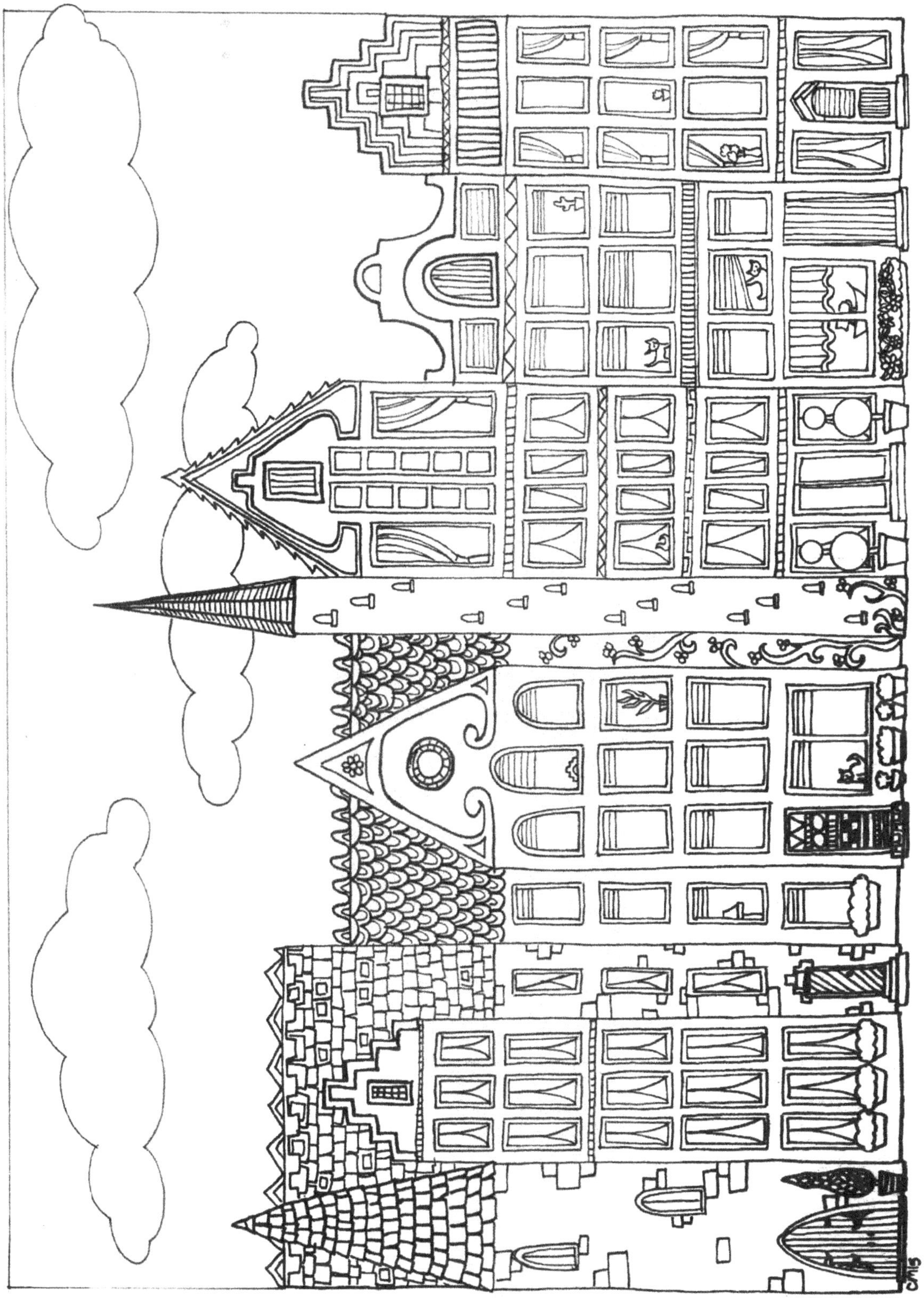

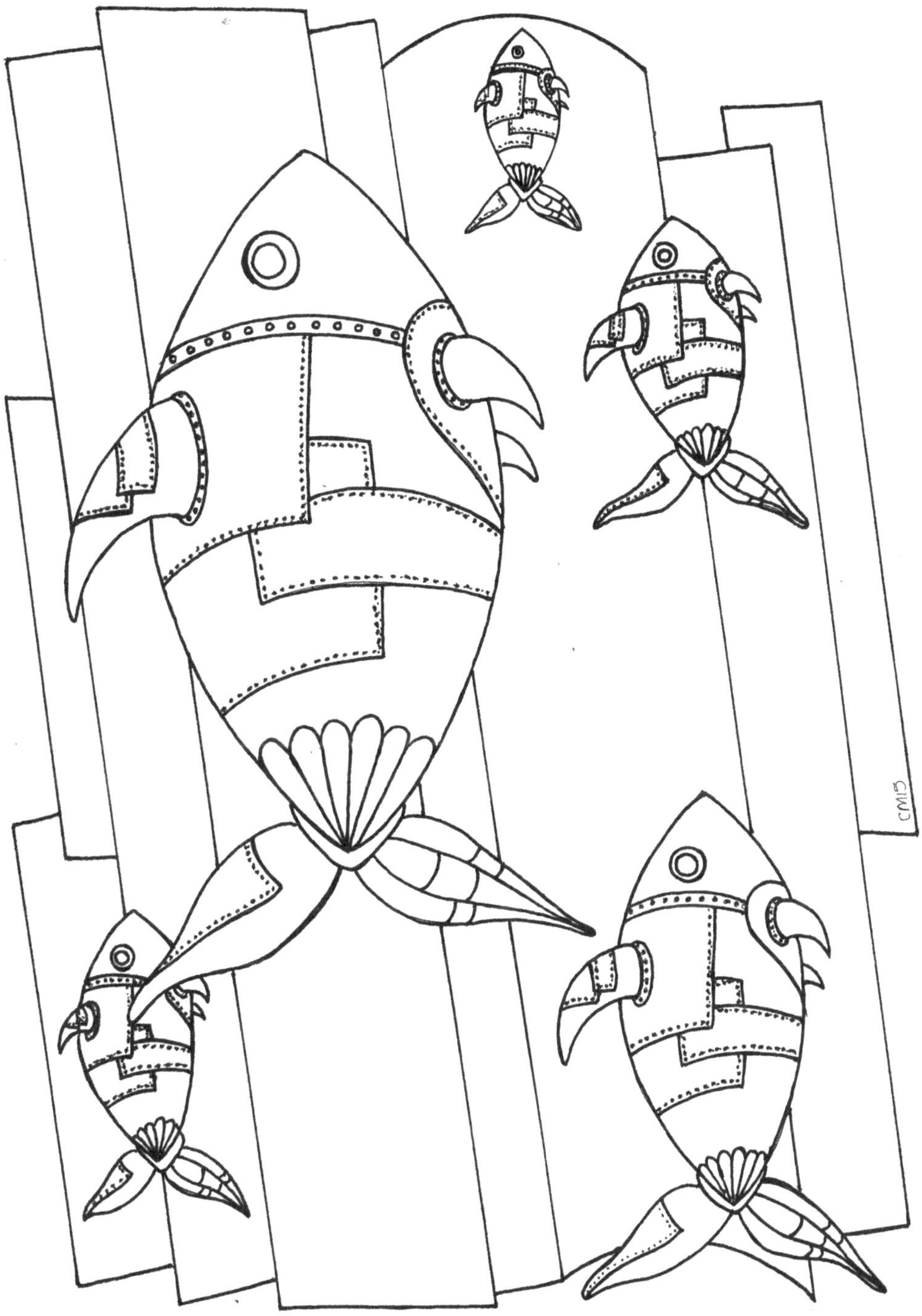

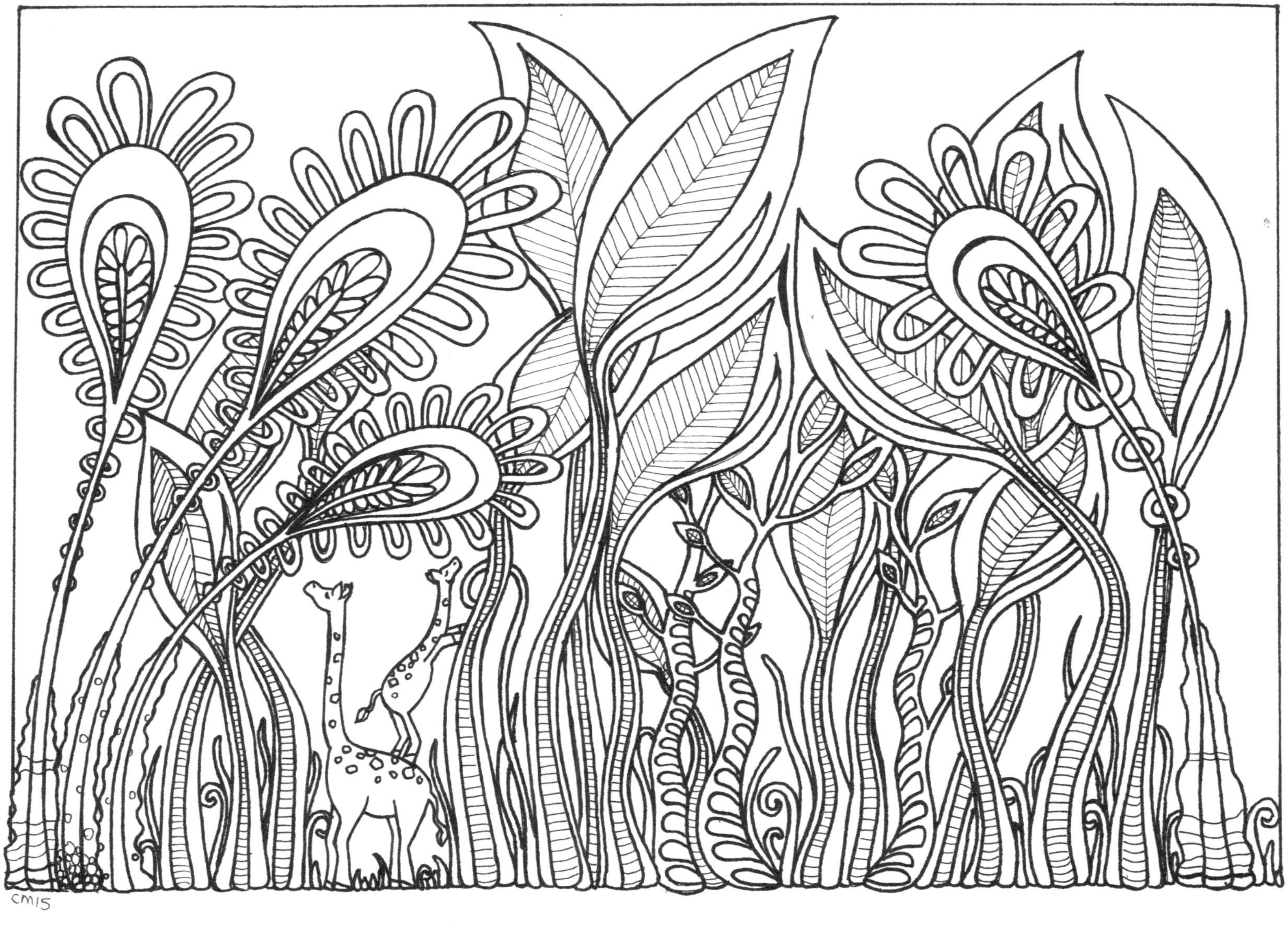
CM15

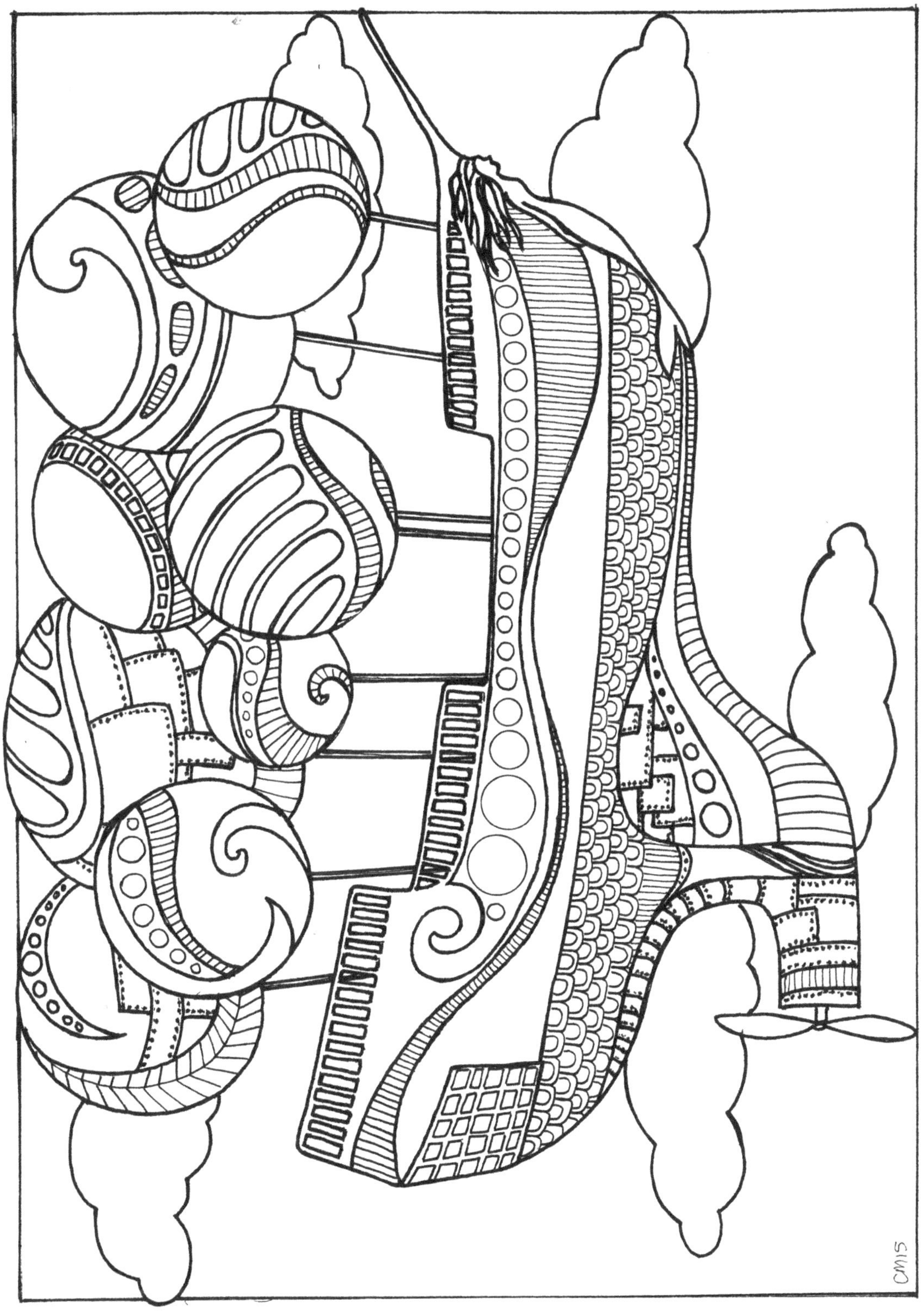
CM15

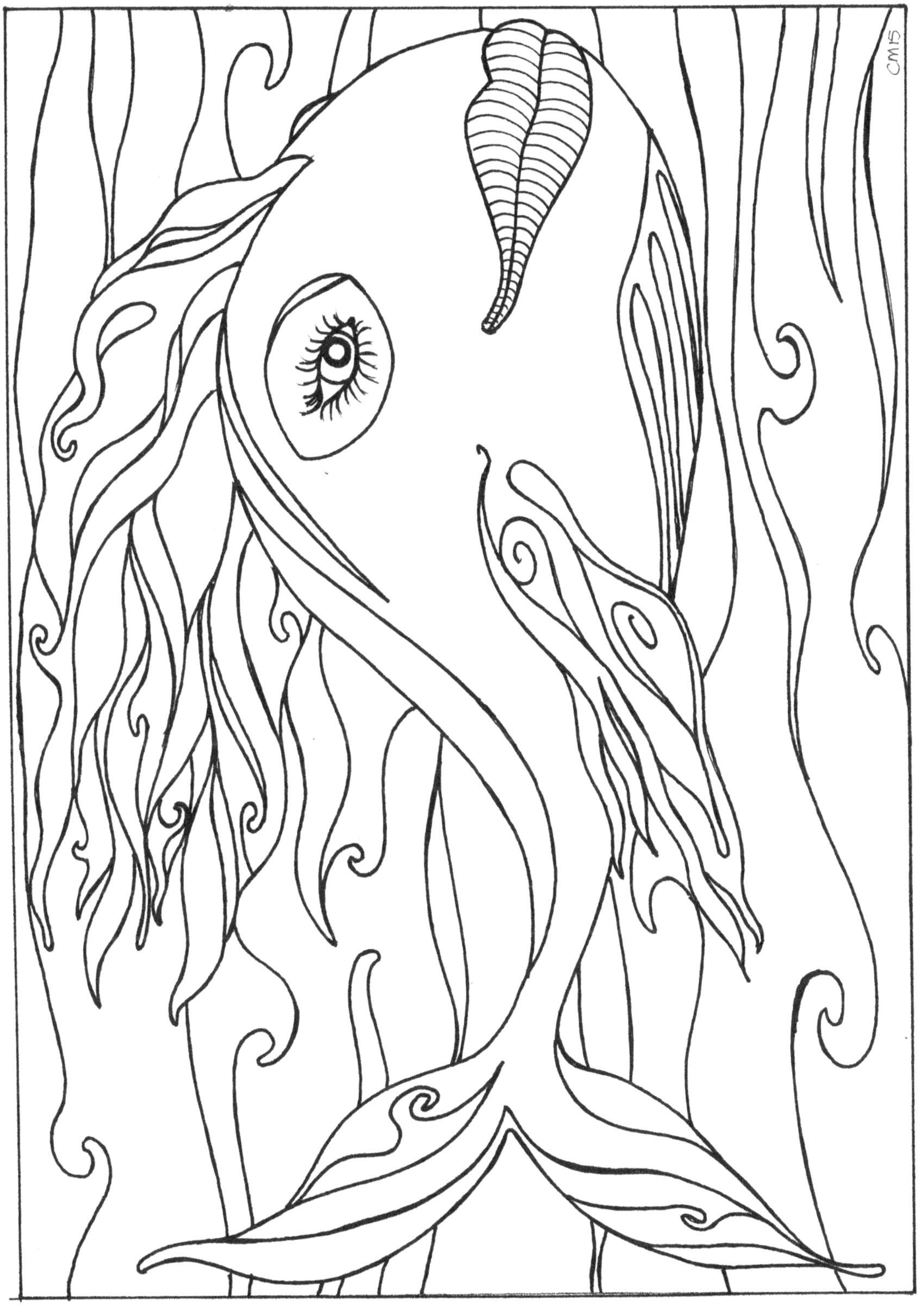

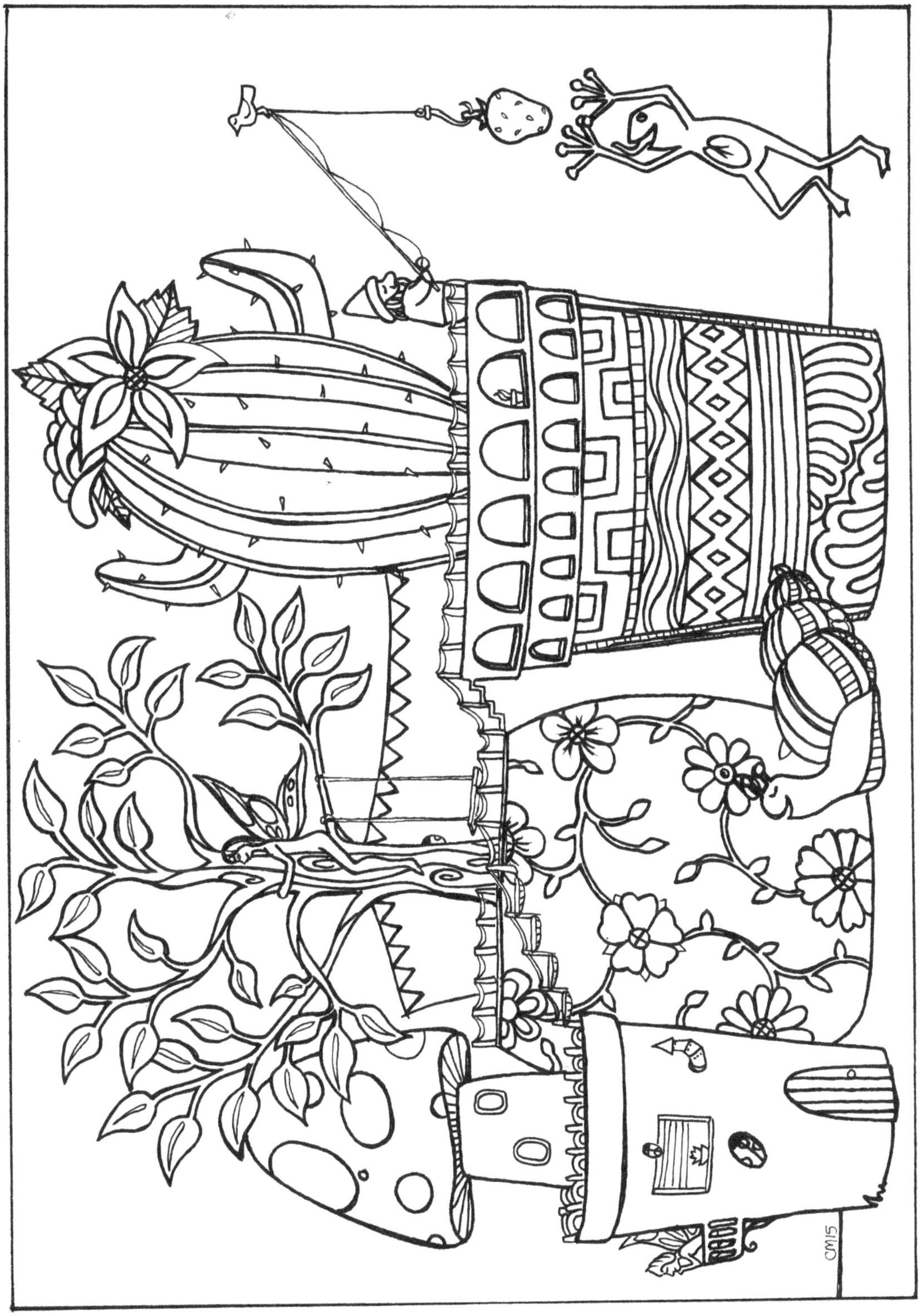

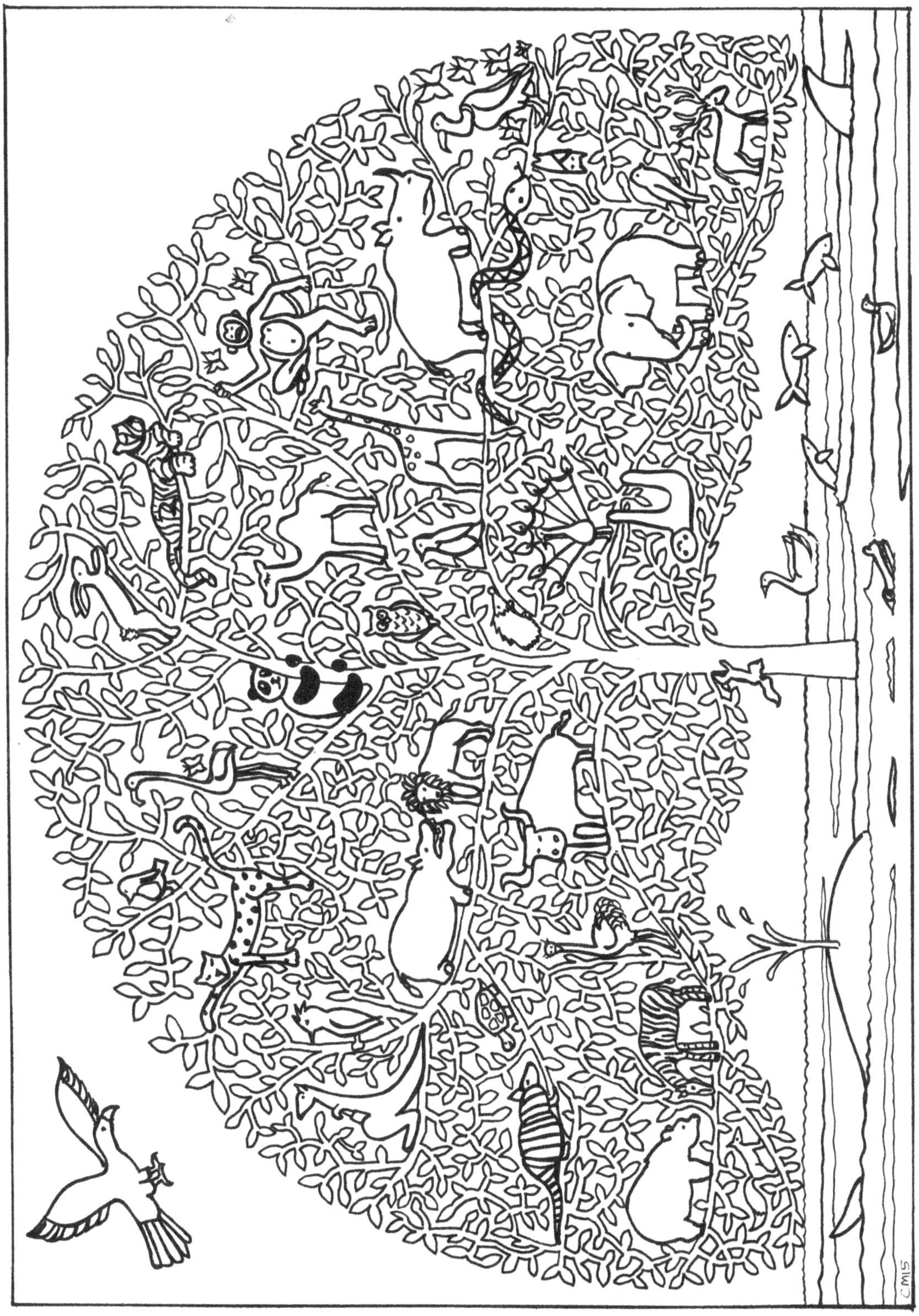

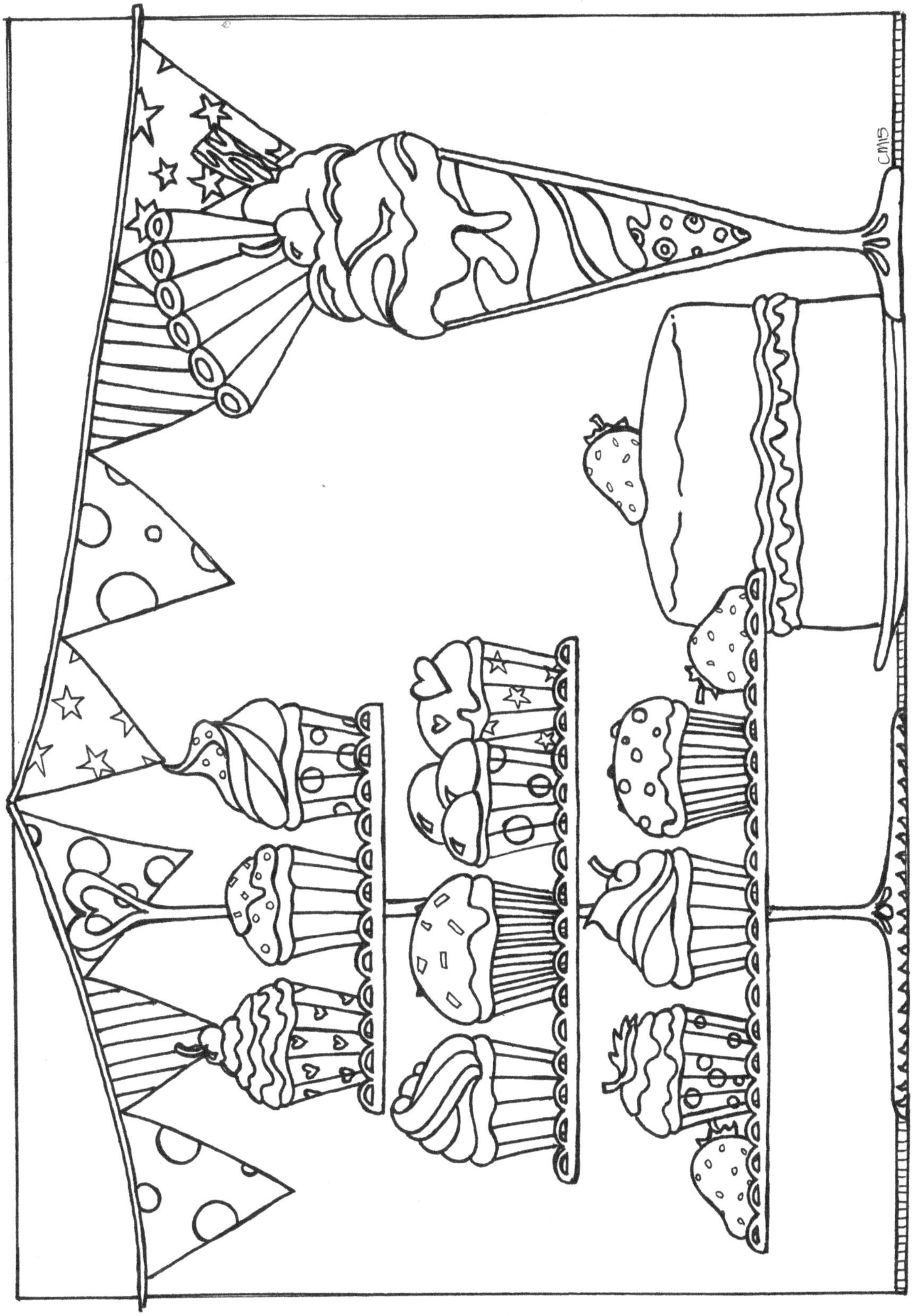

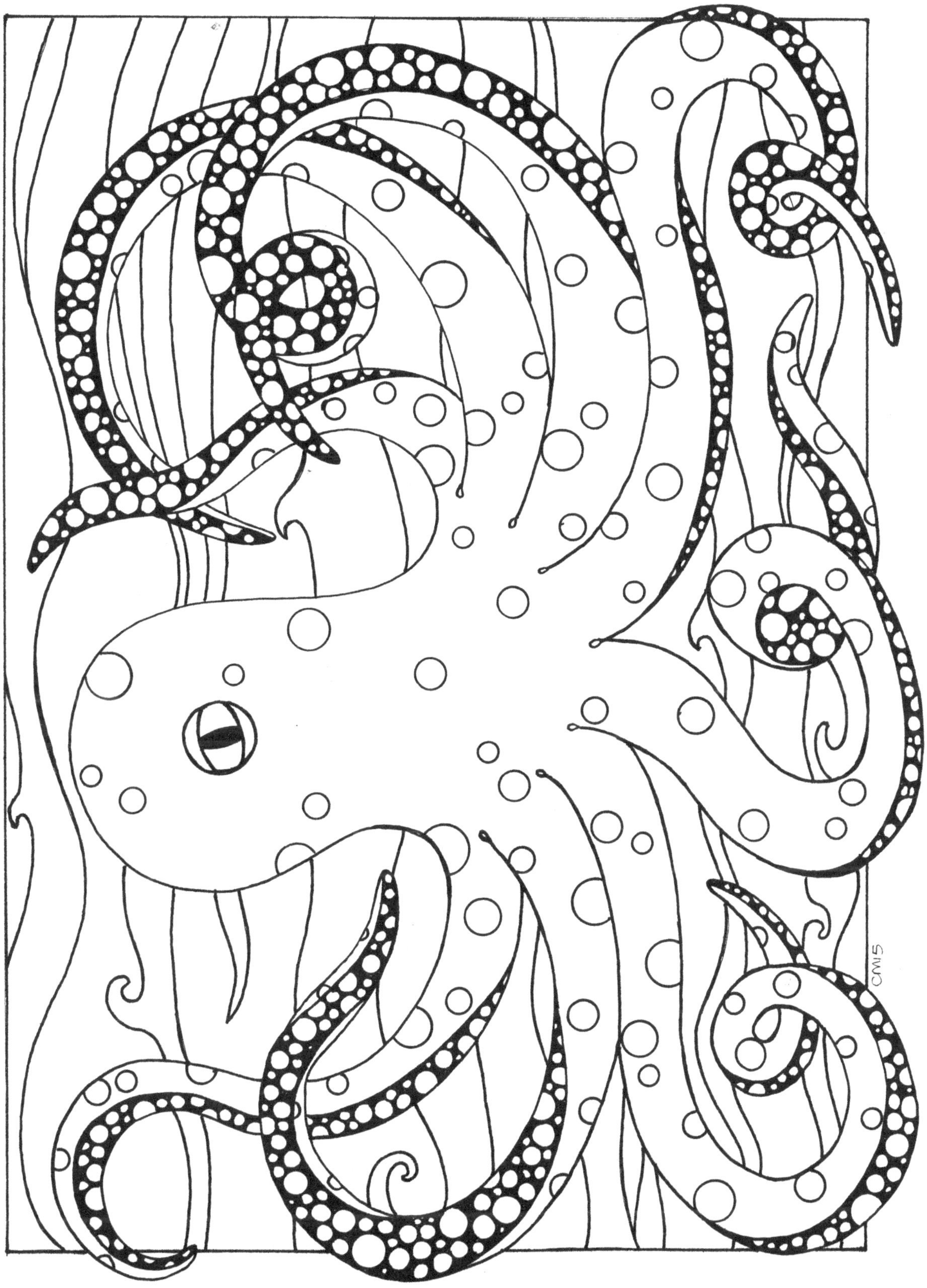

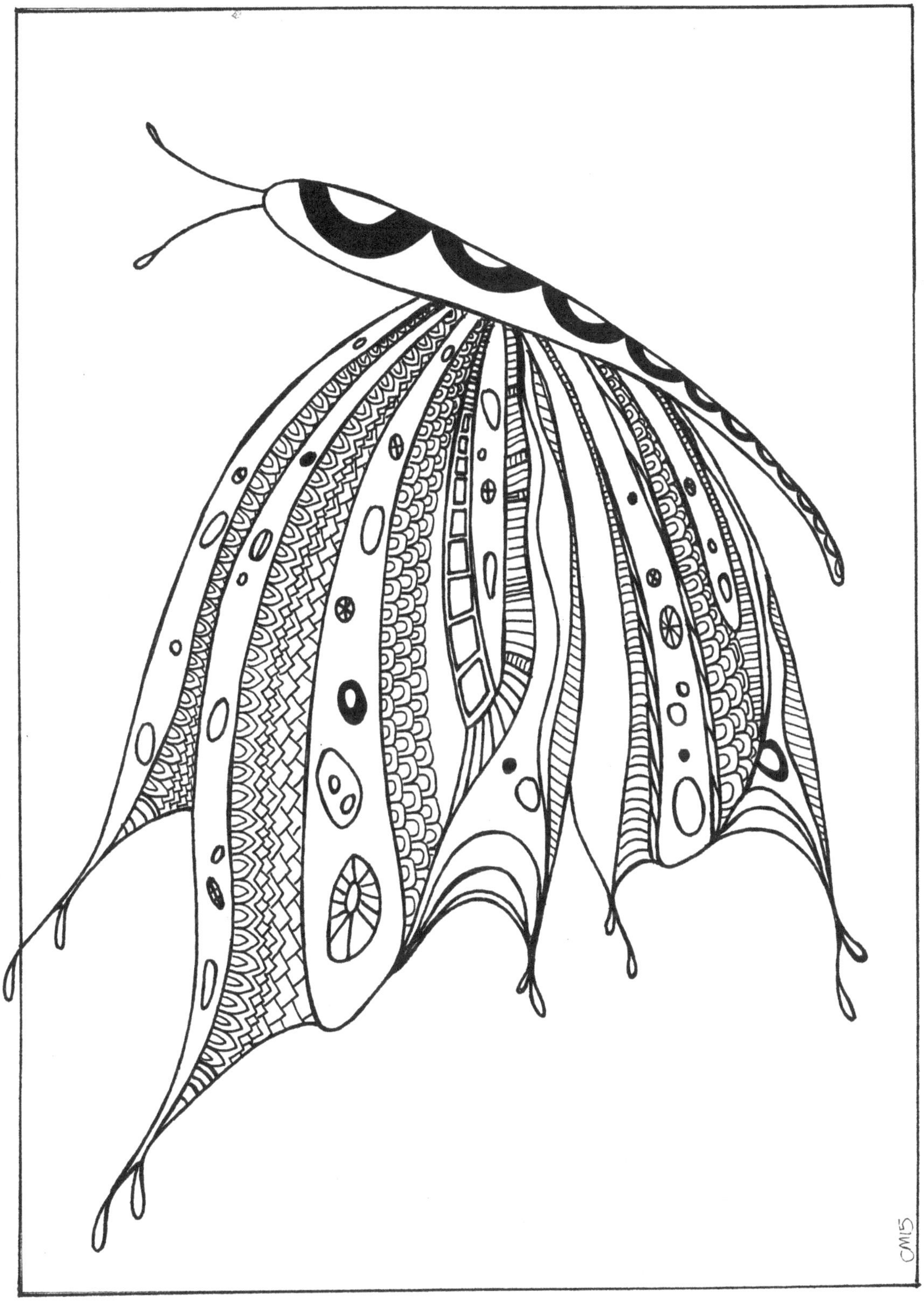
CM15

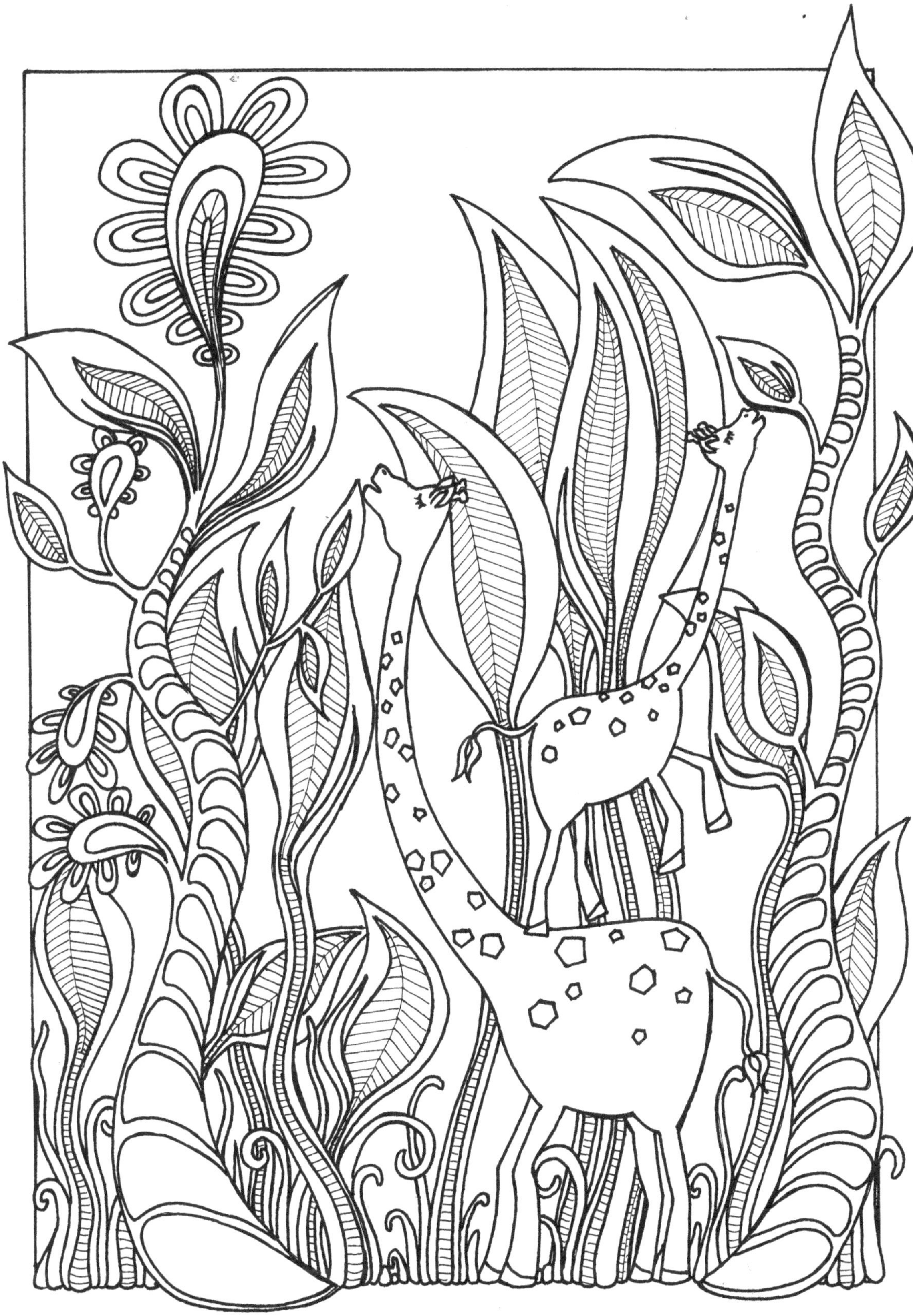

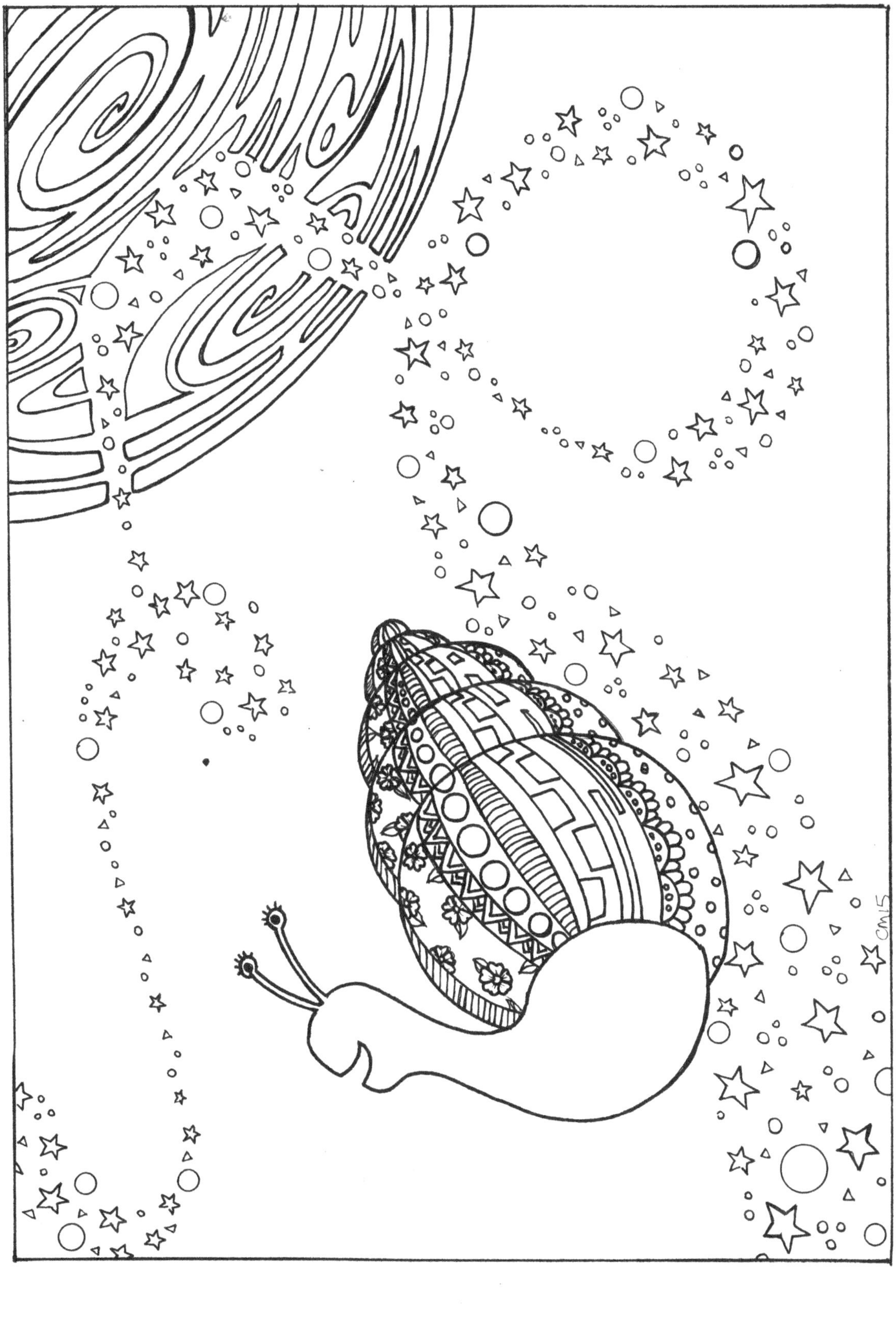
cm15

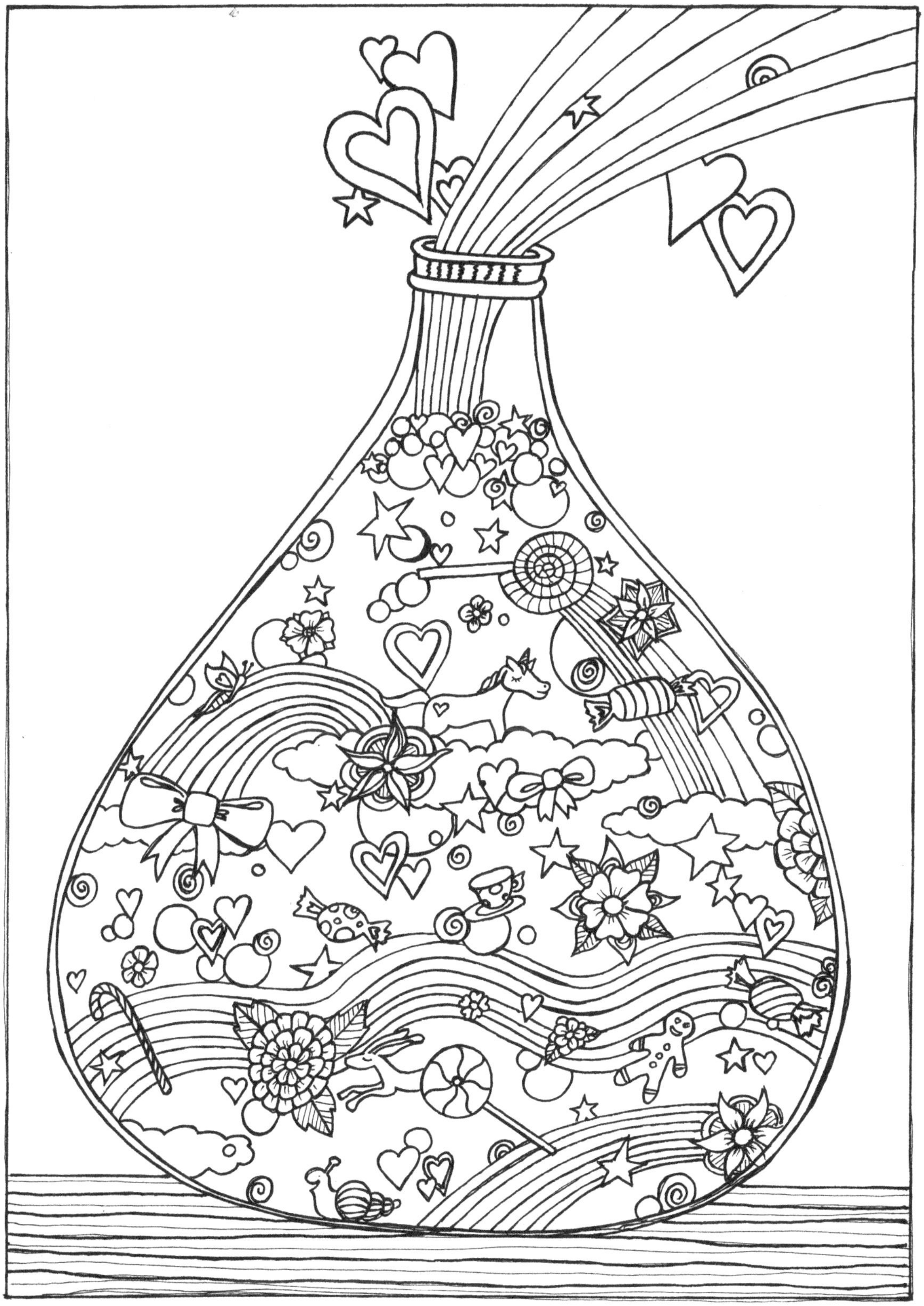

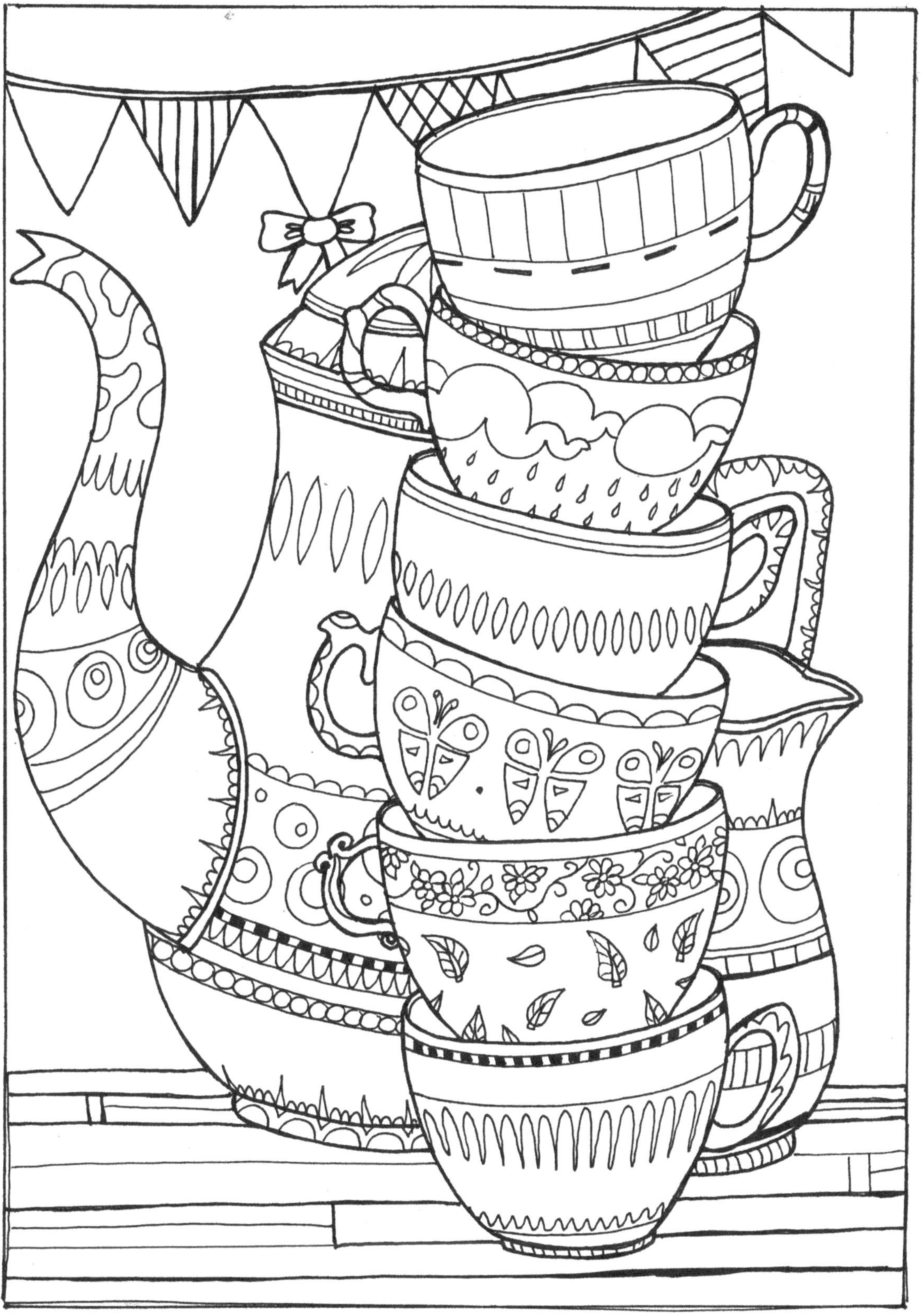

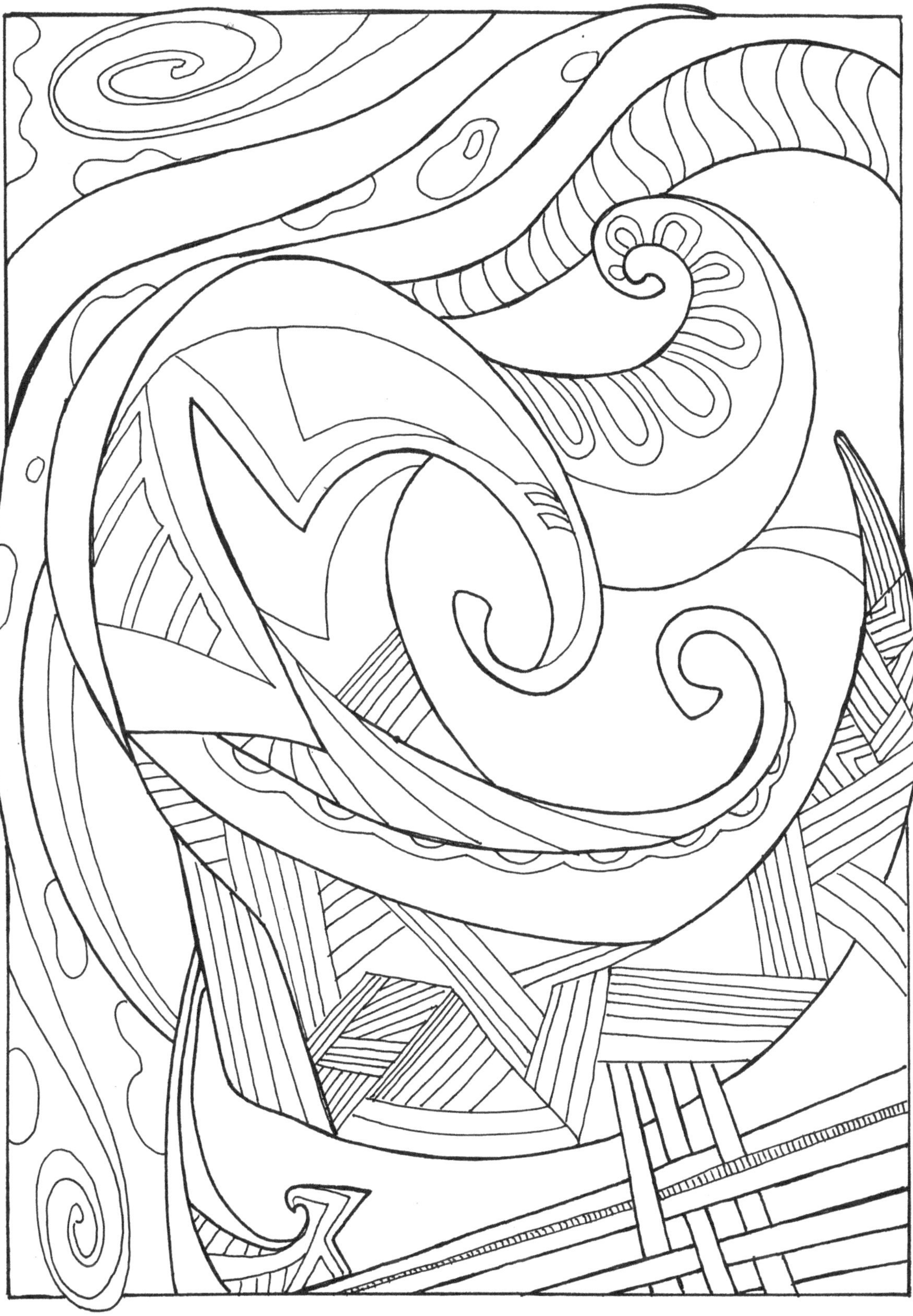

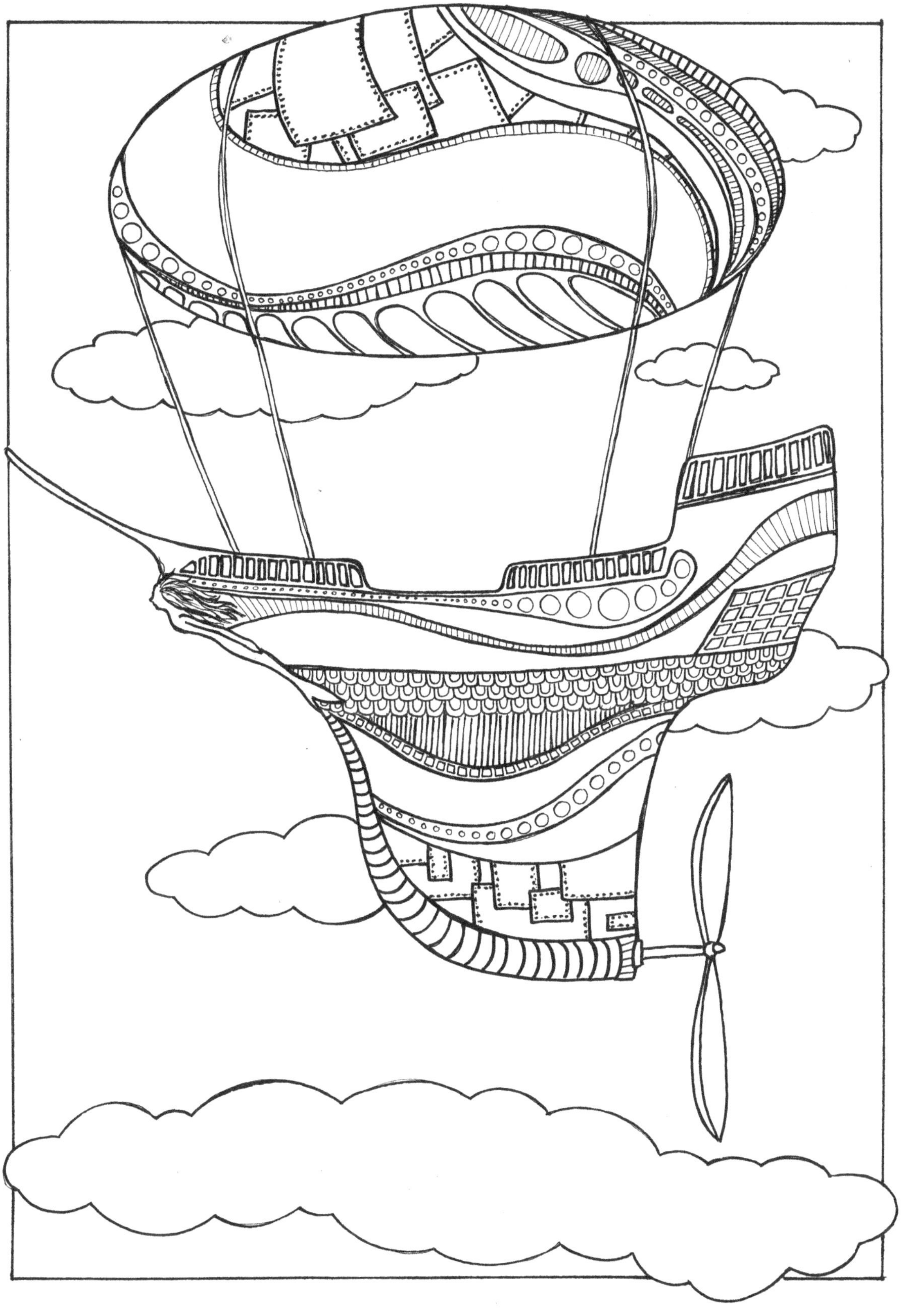

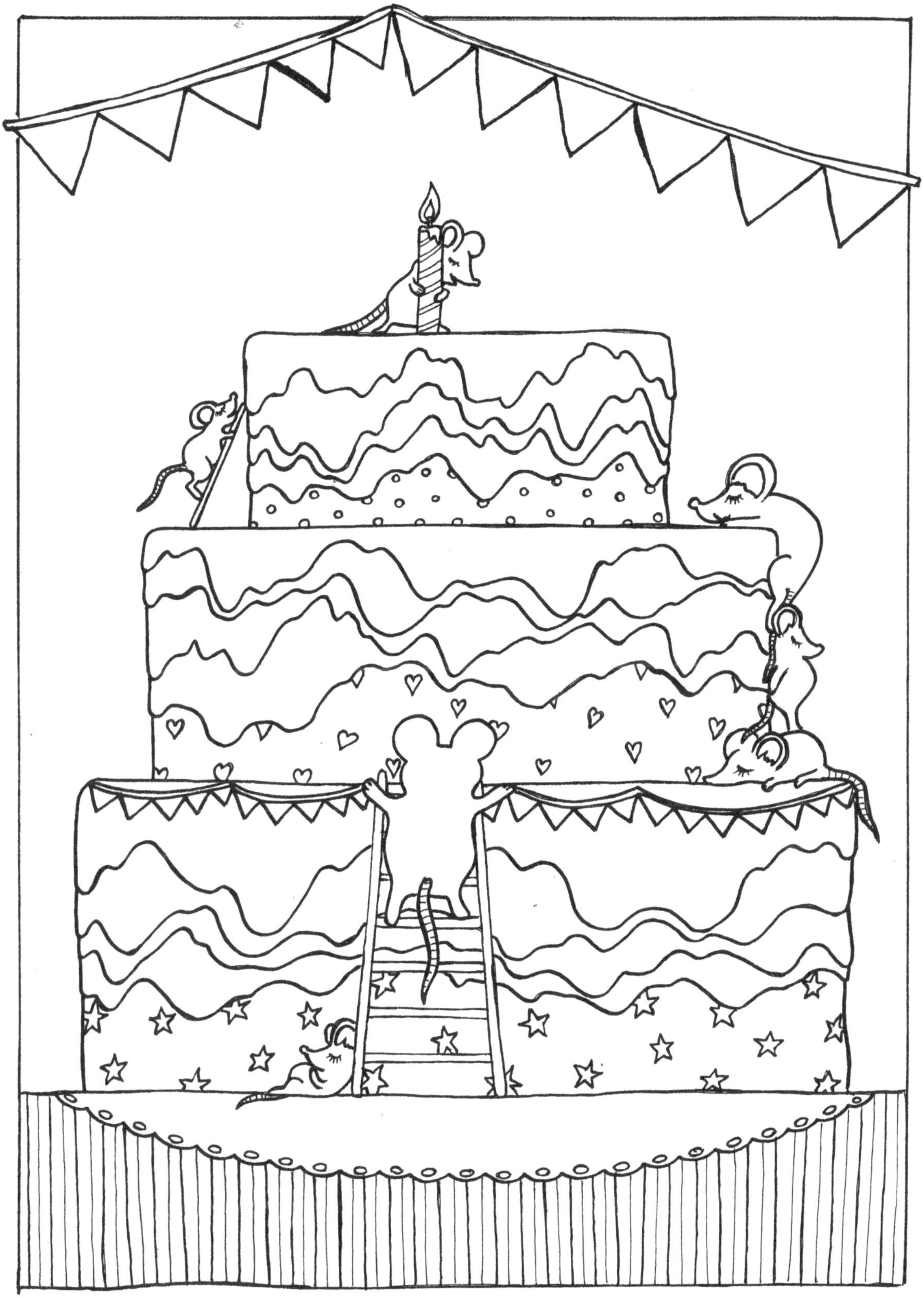

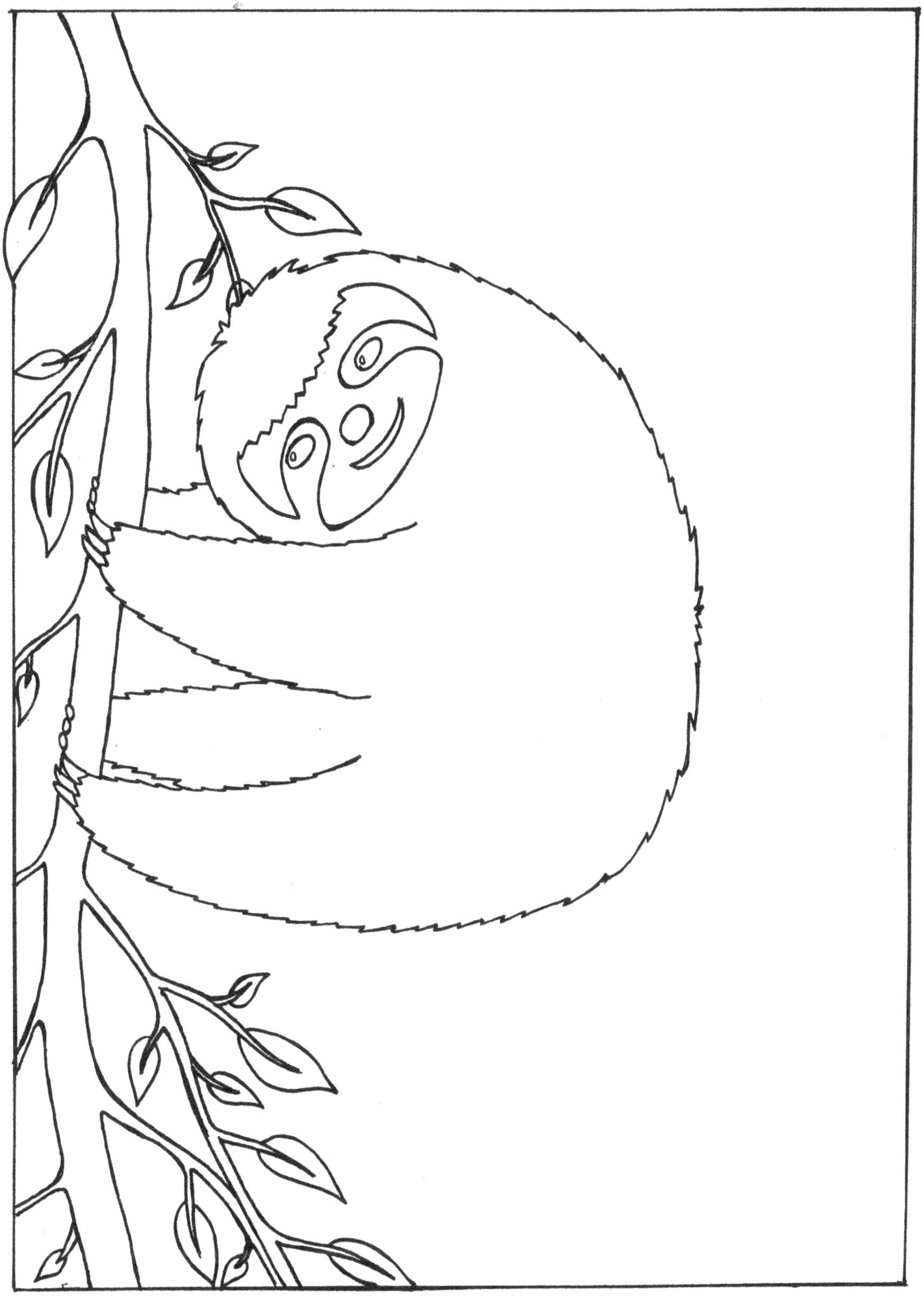

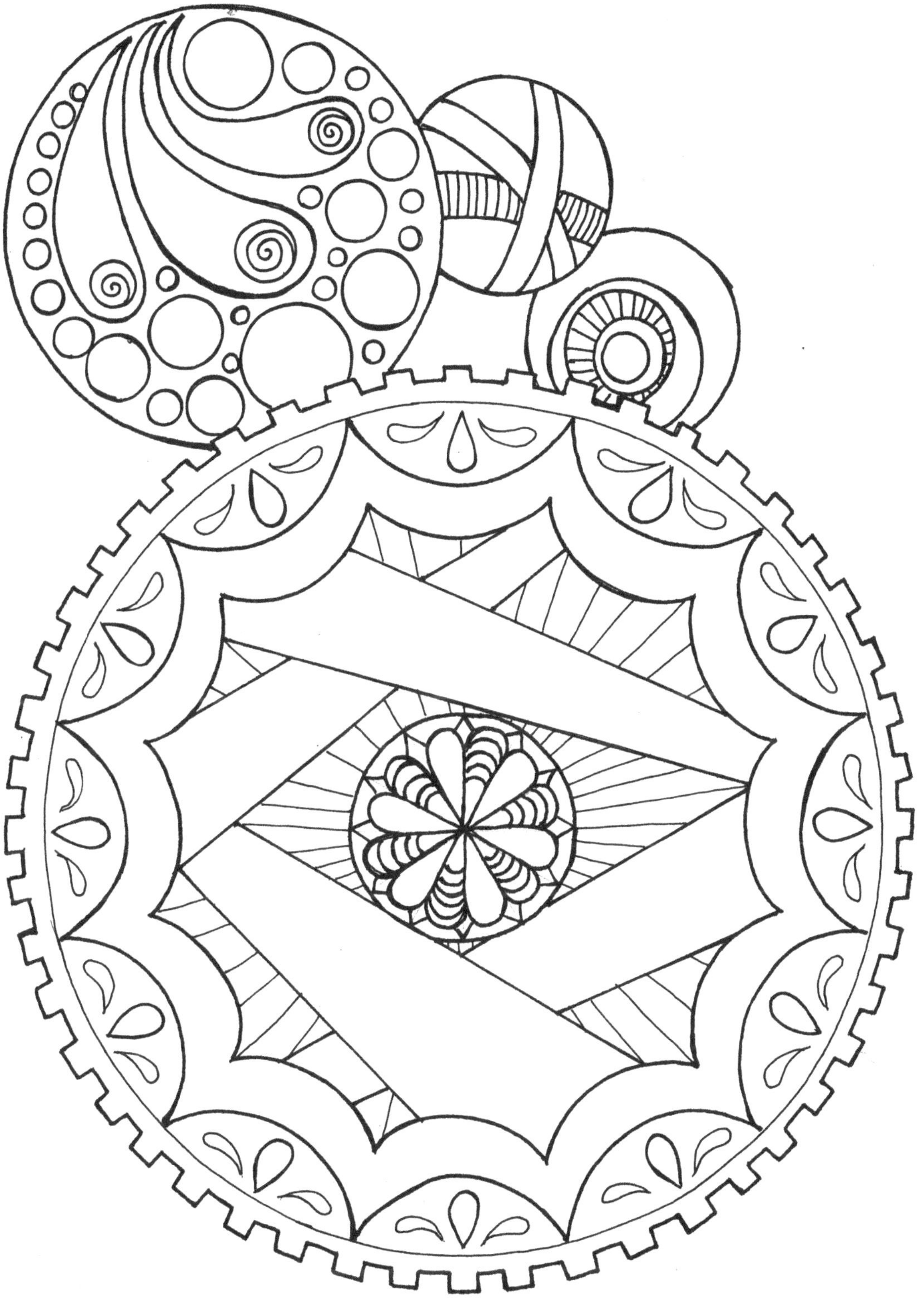

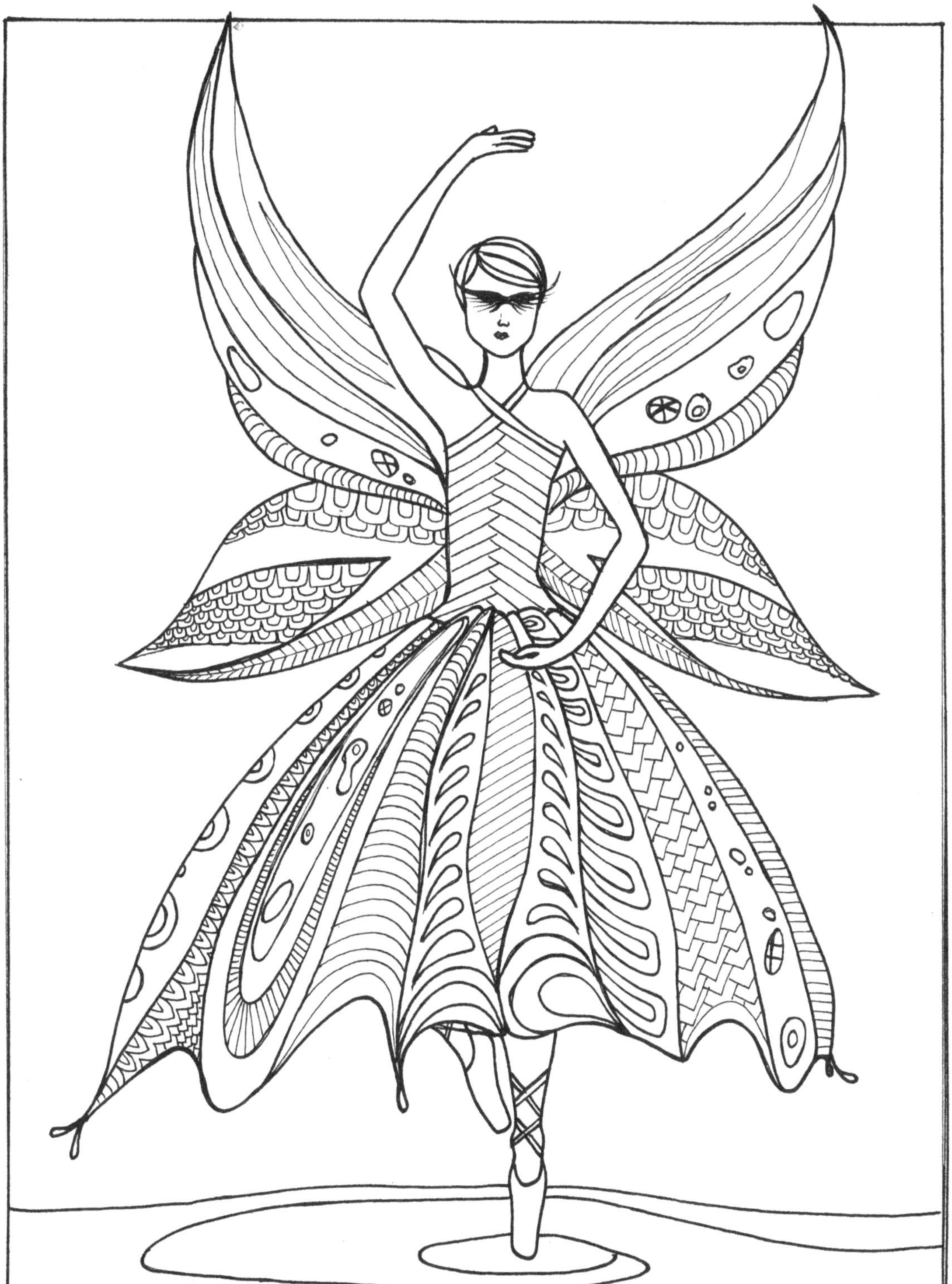

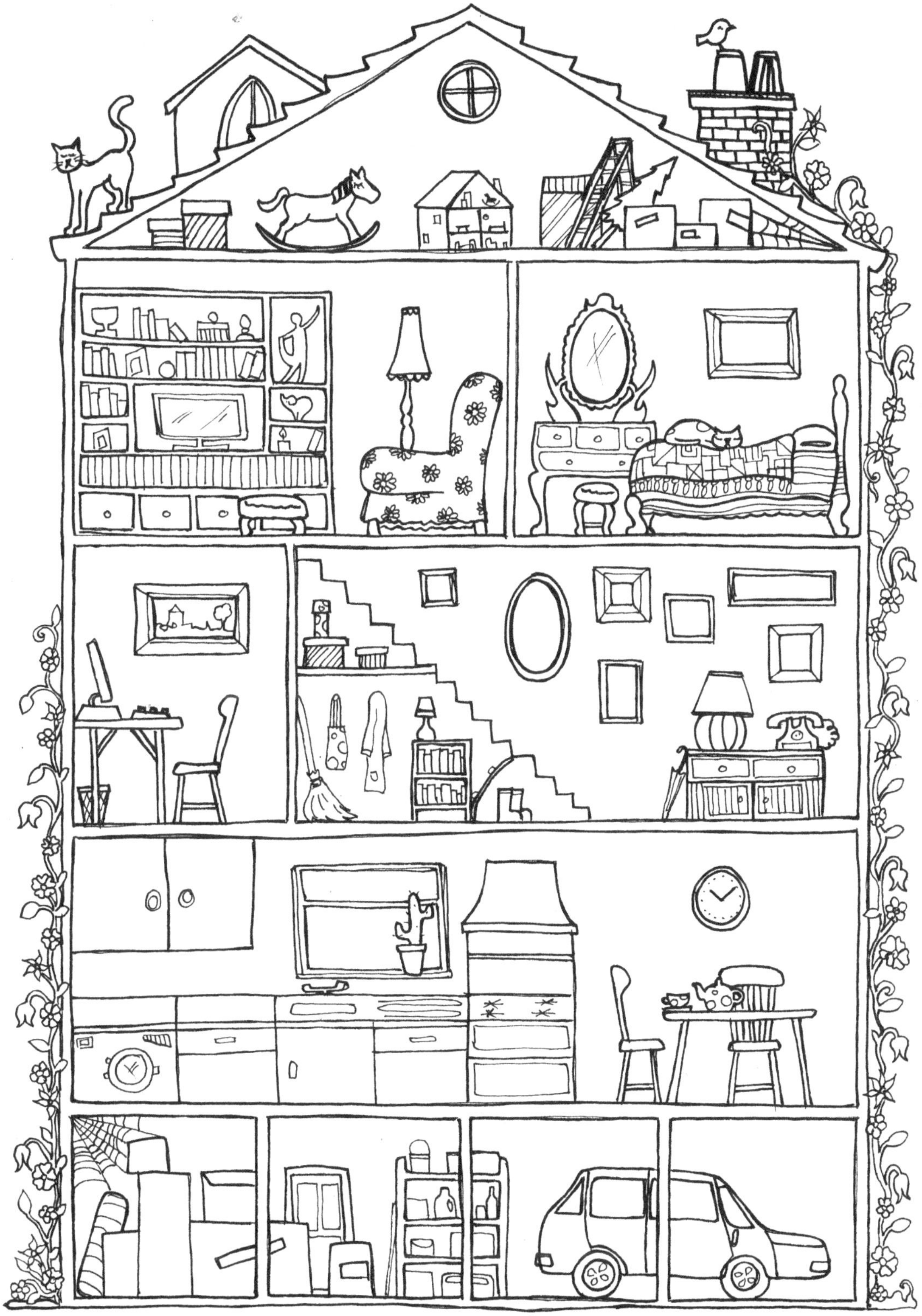

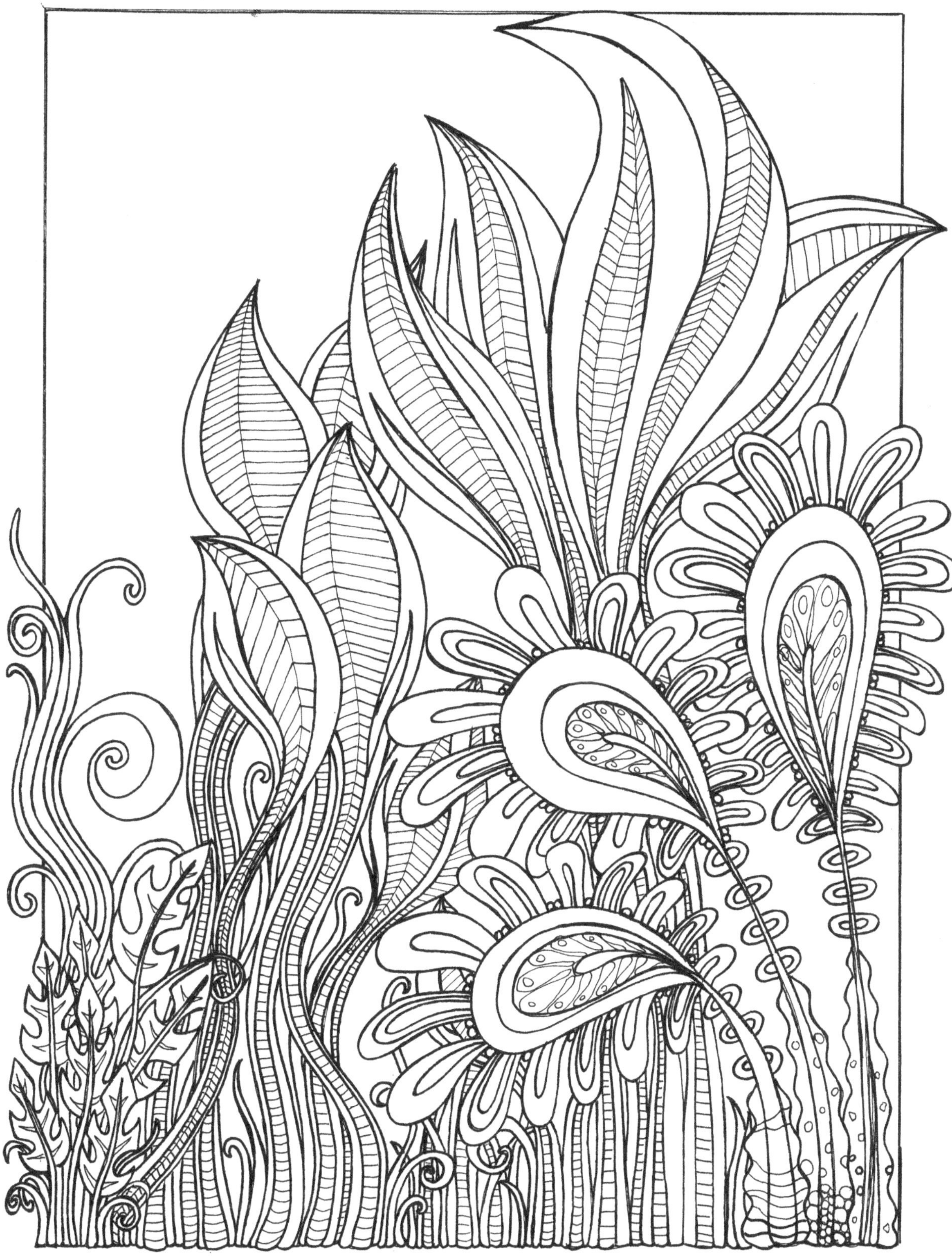

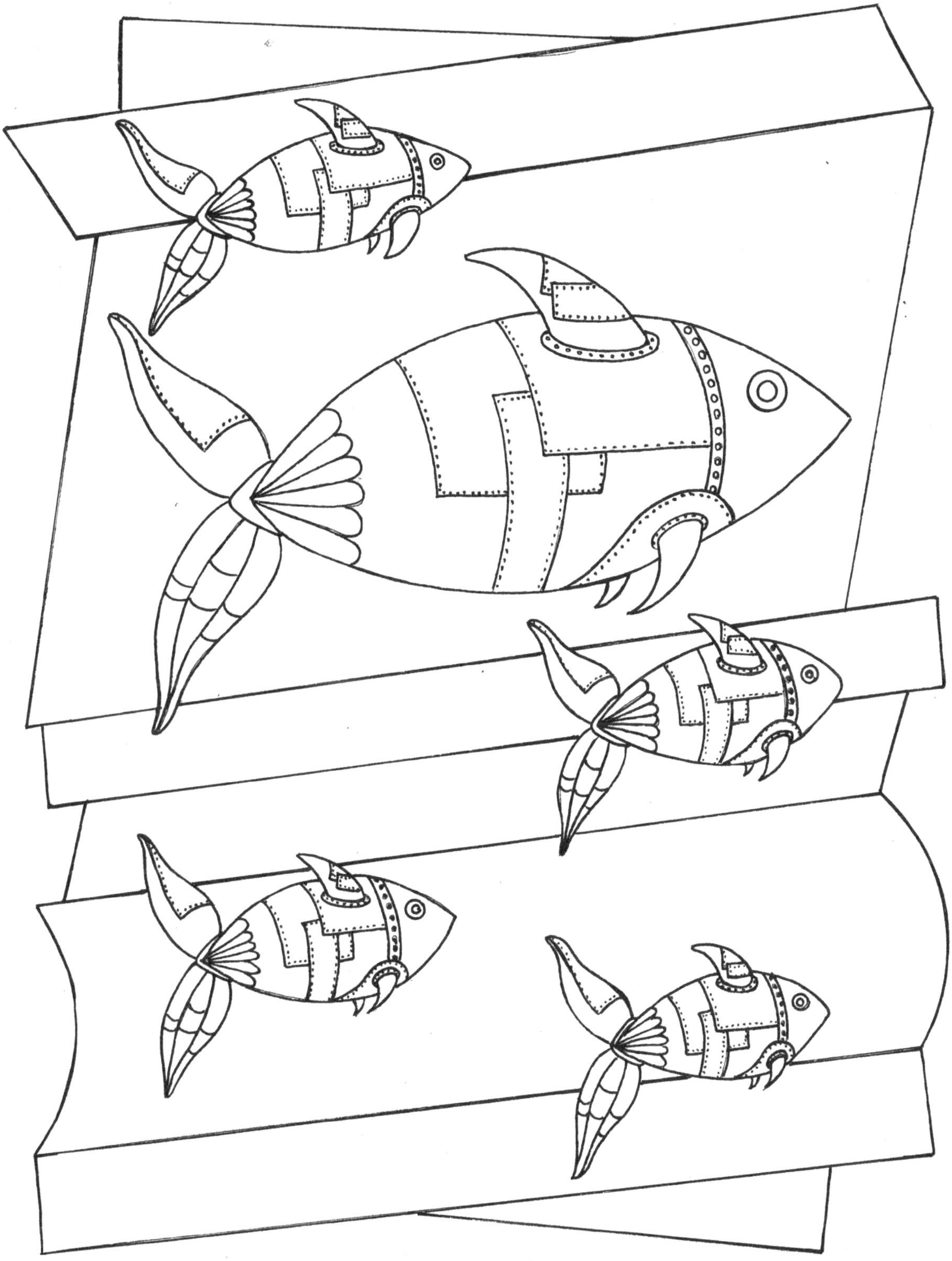

Colour Test Sheet

www.ingramcontent.com/pod-product-compliance
Lightning Source LLC
Chambersburg PA
CBHW081903170526
45167CB00007B/3126
* 9 7 8 1 5 4 2 8 0 5 5 4 4 *